When Spirits Speak

Messages from Spirit Children

May you find your own 7th wave!

Jeri AKA "Writer"

11-11-2011

When Spirits Speak

Messages from Spirit Children

Jeri K. Tory Conklin

7th Wave Publishing
Browns Valley, California

7th Wave Publishing

First printing, October 2011 3468_3

Publisher's Cataloging-in-Publication (Provided by Quality Books, Inc.)

Conklin, Jeri K. Tory.
      When spirits speak: messages from spirit children /
    Jeri K. Tory Conklin.
       p. cm.
       ISBN-13: 978-0-9839387-0-5
       ISBN-10: 0-9839387-0-9

       1. Channeling (Spiritualism) 2. Children~Death.
       3. Spirit writings.   I. Title.

    BF1290.C66 2011   133.9'3
                   QBI11-600182

ISBN-13: 978-0-9839387-0-5

Cover Watercolor © David N. Giles, 2011
Illustration© by Teri Ann "Sunny" Henderson, 2011
Foreword © Marjorie B. Giles, 2011

Published in the United States by 7th Wave Publishing
P.O. Box 282
Browns Valley, California 95918

seventhwavepublishing@yahoo.com

To all those who have crossed over,

but are whispering on the seventh wave

that they are still with us

Contents

Foreword

About half the people in the world believe in reincarnation. Right or wrong need not apply; indeed, they cannot, for neither opinion comes with proof or concrete evidence. While most of us live within the limits of three dimensions, my chosen truth accommodates the possibility of other dimensions, and I believe we're destined to recognize a fourth any day now.

Jeri Tory Conklin is already familiar with other dimensions. Her effortless communications with spirits has led her to prepare *When Spirits Speak: Messages from Spirit Children* in order to share information she has acquired through channeling. Among the spirits who have contacted her are children who have passed on, some in an untimely manner, some not. Each has a loving message and hopes to offer comfort and understanding to those who grieve, believing them lost.

These kids are not lost. No one is. Death is merely an invention of earthborn humans and does not exist in other dimensions. Everyone who ever lived on this planet has returned periodically in the form of some other person, perhaps six or seven times, in order to evolve in spiritual consciousness.

Lots of people hear voices from spirits attempting to communicate. Whoever hears these voices needs to determine whether they come to help or to do harm. The spirit children who approached Jeri evidently come to do good, and we can only benefit from hearing their messages.

It is my opinion that in the world today, the plethora of negative spirit voices is diminishing in power, and enlightening spirit voices, such as those Jeri shares here, are being presented to us with new and expanding wisdom.

Marjorie B. Giles, author of *Under the Plum Tree: The Subconscious Mind*, August 2011

Acknowledgments

There are so many people to thank for allowing this book and dream to become a reality. Someone once said, "It takes a village to raise a child." I believe it takes a village to bring a book to fruition. Listed below are many of those who are part of my village.

First off, to the spirit children who have passed, the greatest *thank you!*

To my mom, Gertrude, and my dad, Doyle, thank you for allowing me to be born to you in this lifetime to experience all that I have; we were perfect matches all along.

To my stepdad, Bob, thank you for taking us all on.

To all my teachers along the way—Diana Siderides, Joan Scott and Joan Anderson, Pamelia Cannataro, Dree Hise McDaniel, Karen Ely and Nancy Hultquist, most of you authors in your own right—you have all impacted my life in a positive and supportive way; thank you.

To Pamela Johnson, my fellow author and friend, thank you for taking me on as a student and believing in my writing ability. Your editing of my rough draft (and it truly was rough) and your assistance with the interior design, was its own seventh wave in action.

To Mia Young, my friend, thank you for your continued support and encouragement and for holding your vision of this finished book when my own dream was failing.

To the Backroom Writing Group—Yvonne, Jani, and Stephanie—thank you for believing in my work and offering your support, critical feedback and encouragement.

To Marjorie Giles, without your belief in what I do and who I am, without your encouragement and inspiration, this book would still be in a binder sitting on my shelf.

To David Giles, thank you for your own spirit child coming through for my beautiful watercolor cover.

To Teri Ann "Sunny" Henderson (my own talented and gifted daughter), thank you for the beautiful illustration that graces the dedication page of this book. You are so loved.

To my siblings, Stan, Candy and Sue, I love you all.

To my Aunt Audrey, thank you for taking time to read this book in its manuscript form, as well as all my other stories. I truly appreciate your honesty and your belief in what I do.

To my husband, Kurt, thank you for your belief in my ability to write and publish this book. Your eyes and the way you've expertly smoothed over the transitions and helped with the design have been invaluable.

To Amy Rost, my editor, thank you for polishing the following words to bring out the shine.

To anyone along this journey that I have forgotten to mention, thank you for the lessons along the way and being part of my village.

And to the sea, my forever friend, thank you for the seventh wave.

Introduction

One, two, three, four, five, six . . .

I had come to Cape Cod in 2007, a week after my last radiation treatment to spend time on the beach healing from breast-cancer surgery. Something had to change in my life, and I had come here to figure out what those changes might be.

"Count the waves," my friend Pamelia had said before I'd left Weatherford, Texas. "God always sends the answer you seek on the seventh wave."

So there I sat, counting waves. And on every seventh wave, I seemed to receive information about lifestyle and attitude changes I needed to make. But then I heard something that wasn't about me.

One, two, three, four, five, six . . .

"Hello," a small voice called. "Writer, I'm Aaron. Can you hear me?"

I glanced around, but saw no one—just the usual morning fog hugging the coastline.

"Writer, I'm Aaron," the voice said again. "Can you hear me?"

"Yes, I can hear you," I said, realizing where the small voice had come from.

It had been a number of years since I had last connected with children in the world of spirit. I had begun communicating with them not long after I was born. I never questioned my ability to speak with or see spirit children—children whose spirits had, at their death, left their bodies and this physical dimension and moved into the next, nonphysical dimension. I just didn't understand why adults didn't see or hear them. Then, when I was ten, my father was killed, and I shut down my communication with the world of spirit.

In 1996, as an adult, I began to allow spirit communication back into my life when I connected with two earthbound spirit children at my home in Idaho. But it wasn't until that day I sat on the beach in Cape Cod, counting the waves, and seeking change and healing that I realized communicating with the world of spirit *and* sharing those messages with others must be a way back to living the life I was meant to live. So I listened.

"Will you write a letter to my parents?" Aaron asked. "I want to tell them I'm okay, I made it home, and I'm safe."

I saw a group of spirit children lining up in front of me.

"We all want you to write for us," another voice added. "Will you, writer, will you?"

"Sure," I said, pen in hand.

It was to be a long day, with lots of writing, as I started counting spirit children instead of waves. The children came to me in their own order. I wrote down each of their letters as I received it and put it in my notebook. I did not realize until I began typing up the letters that not only had the kids arranged themselves in near alphabetical order, but also that the causes of their passing were different. (The word "passing" here means physical death. The physical body expires; the soul and spirit live on. The children themselves use the terms "death," "dying," and "passing" in their letters.) The majority of letters came through while I was sitting on the beach. When I ran out of paper in my tablet, I returned home for more and there received the remaining letters. Then, as I began typing the letters for this book in 2011, more children, who had passed after 2007, came to me with their letters. Some of those children gave me messages for their loved ones, and some shared just messages in general.

I learned many lessons from those spirit children, and I give to you their letters in the book you now hold, for several reasons.

First, I believe my work with spirit children is inspired by a higher power, which I know as "God." Bringing forth their letters in a published format is my way of saying, "I am a communicator with the world of spirit. This is who I am, and what I do."

Second, as our soul moves into an ever-widening spiritual evolution, I believe it is important to see in written form more and more accounts of communication with the world of spirit. It is time for others to realize that this communication is possible.

Finally, I believe that God speaks to and through each of us in many different ways—including through the voices of those in the world of spirit—in an attempt to remind us of the spiritual home we all left behind when our spirits chose to incarnate in physical bodies in this physical dimension. This book of letters and stories will, I hope, inspire *faith* by showing that there is a god in heaven, waiting for us to return home; *hope*, by showing that there is life after the passing of the physical body; and the knowledge that *love* knows no bounds, as our loved ones come back to tell us they are safe and with us still in spirit, if not in body. If you have lost a loved one or one of the children included in this book is related to you, please know that they are safe and with God. This is what the spirit children who spoke with me on the beach have come to tell us. This is not my message, but theirs.

I pray you are one of these children's loved ones and, in reading this book, find your way to your son or daughter's letter. If not, perhaps you know of someone who needs to hear the messages and will pass this book on.

The spirits of the children who came to me at Cape Cod had all gone "home"; when their physical bodies had died, their spirits had crossed over into the nonphysical dimension, which some of them refer to as heaven. But they were able to reach back into the physical realm in order to talk to me. Not every spirit makes that transition—or at least not right away. Such is the case with the *earthbound* spirit children I've encountered. Although their spirits had left their bodies when their bodies died, those spirits had not left yet the physical plane; at the time I met them, they had not yet gone home to the world of spirit. (I prefer not to call them "ghosts," for they truly were spirit children, left behind or staying behind in this world for some reason.)

I have included the stories of my encounters with them to demonstrate that not all spirits immediately go home to be with God, but remain earthbound until they decide to make the transition. These stories also demonstrate how I experienced interacting with these spirit children while they were on the physical plane. While I was able to see the spirit children who brought forth letters on Cape Cod, I did not have the same type of physical interaction with them as I did with the earthbound spirit children.

Just as I am reclaiming my gift for speaking with those in the world of spirit, it is time for others to discover that they too have the same gift. Though this is not a how-to book, I begin with some basic information about how this type of communication works. It is my hope that as you read these letters and stories, you will realize your own gift for speaking to those you know who have passed over into the world of spirit.

I have also added a question-and-answer section at the end of this book for those readers, who may, after having read this book, seek answers of their own. I sought out questions for the spirit children through a social-network website and was amazed at the many questions I received. The questions are varied, and some were of a personal nature from the questioner. To answer these questions, the spirit children appeared as a group once again, but instead of answering as individual children, they spoke as a collective conscious. I was amazed at the depth of their answers to questions that to me seemed beyond the maturity of the children. All in all, their answers demonstrate the ability of those within the world of spirit to ferret out the question behind the question and provide an answer.

1

Communicating With the World of Spirit

*All beings, whether seen or unseen, have the ability to communicate
with and understand each other.*

The means by which I communicate with spirit children
probably most resembles what we think of as telepathy, or
communication directly between one mind and another,
without any words being spoken.

Telepathic communication has been going on in
different cultures since the beginning of time as we know it.
Considered a universal language, it is shared by all as
inhabitants of Mother Earth. Before there was a vocal
spoken language, telepathic communication—or "mind talk,"
as I call it—is all there was. During a time when I was truly
wondering how I was able to easily share information with
people without opening my mouth, I stumbled upon John
Wyndham's book *Rebirth*, a story about nonspeaking
mutants trying to rebuild a shattered civilization. While
Rebirth is a work of fiction, the application of mental
telepathy as a means of communication reminded me that
telepathy has been demonstrated within indigenous cultures

everywhere. After reading Wyndham's work, I finally understood: telepathy is possible. This knowledge has helped me throughout my journey and saved my life many times over. In addition to having the potential to communicate telepathically, each and every one of us came into this lifetime knowing that we could communicate with entities from the "other side." When we are young children, the veil between the spirit home we have just left and our new, earthly home is thin. Not only do we communicate with those we leave behind, but our soul also moves freely between the two dimensions. If we are born into a family that accepts our communication with animals and spirits, then we are encouraged and supported. If not, then we bow to social and parental pressures, wrapping our knowledge in oilskin and tucking it away in our secret box where it will be safe until we can use it again.

Communication from those in the world of spirit comes to us in several different ways. The three most common ways are:

> **Clairvoyance (visual communication),** which allows us to see thoughts or information, not necessarily with our physical eyes, but rather as colors, forms, and textures in our mind's eye (also known as the third eye).

> **Clairaudience (auditory communication),** which allows us to hear thoughts or receive information

not with our physical ears, but as voices in our minds.

Clairsentience (tactile communication), in which we pick up thoughts and information and convert them into a feeling, be it emotional or physical. You may feel the information as calming feelings, as a prickly sensation, or as the hairs on your arms and back of your neck standing up. As you begin to differentiate the types of spiritual energies you are dealing with, you will come to recognize the different feelings each triggers for you. For example, when I am in the presence of a spiritual entity, my legs begin to tingle.

I communicate with the world of spirit primarily through clairvoyance and clairaudience. I don't physically hear voices speaking out loud; rather, I hear spirits' thoughts translated into words. I believe this type of communication is similar to, if not the same as, telepathy, in which all communication is exchanged through thought. When I speak with spirit children, I hear what they are saying as clearly as I hear people in ordinary reality speaking. The voices of the spirits I hear sound just like those of people I speak with in regular conversations, but I hear these voices within my head.

Communication with the world of spirit can be done any time, any place. It doesn't require anything other than for you to show up and ask questions with respect and appreciation. Communicating with spiritual beings—whether they are angels and fairies, the spirits of children who have died, or the spirits of rocks or trees—is as simple as sitting quietly and allowing yourself to hear or see what they would have you know. Their voices are, quite simply the still, small voice you hear in your head, see in your mind's eye, or feel with your body or emotions.

2
Earthbound Spirit Children

The children whose stories you are about to read were earthbound spirits—the spirits of children who had died, but instead of "crossing over" to the world of spirit, stayed within the physical, earthly plane. A spirit might choose to remain earthbound for any number of reasons. If the person's death is sudden and unexpected, the spirit can become confused and doesn't know how to accept that he or she has died. Perhaps something catches the spirit's attention at that crucial moment, and it doesn't make the transition. Or maybe the spirit feels it needs to stay behind on earth for its family and loved ones. In some cases, the spirit just isn't ready to cross over, for whatever reason. In many cases, the spirit believes itself to still be physically alive.

I had learned early on, when I first encountered Mary, one of the spirit children I've lived with, how to help earthbound spirits transition, cross over, or go home. I do so by offering them the Light, meaning the light from heaven or the world of spirit, which opens what I call the rainbow bridge, the path between this physical dimension and the nonphysical dimension. I often see the Light as rays of sunshine streaming down from the skies. Since Mary, I have helped several earthbound spirit children find their way home to the world of spirit.

Jamie and Mary

Once I had outgrown childhood and reopened my communication with the world of spirit, my experiences of seeing and interacting with that world evolved. As I branched out into different fields of work with the world of spirit, I had more interaction with the adult spirits, and I deeply missed the spirit children I had known as a child. So I was excited to have two spirit children, Jamie and Mary, come into my life when my family and I moved to Idaho in 1992.

Our property bordered the Oregon Trail, with its history of wagon trains moving west upon its rutted dirt road, and perhaps that proximity is what gave rise to the extra spirit activity in this place. Oftentimes at night, when all was still and the moon full, we could hear the turn of invisible wagon wheels and the methodical plodding of long-dead oxen driving through the night. On occasion, we even heard singing coming from a ghostly wagon train as it rolled by.

Jamie, 1995

Jamie first appeared in my sight on Christmas Eve, 1995. My husband, Kurt, was in Iceland for a year, and I had put up a small Christmas tree with lots of twinkle lights and handmade Christmas balls. Under the tree there were a couple of wrapped gifts from my family and a few for my daughter, Teri Ann, who had moved out that year. Hearing the balls on the tree tinkling, I got up to investigate, suspecting that one of the cats was batting at the balls and the tree would be on the floor soon. Instead, there stood Jamie, shaking one of the presents. He appeared to be around twelve years old and was dressed in ratty cotton pajamas.

As startled as I was to see him, he was even more startled that I *could* see him. I believe the people who lived there prior to us were not aware of Jamie's existence, so he moved freely around the property.

"It's okay," I said to him. "Don't go."

Like two magnets both facing north, positive ends facing, we circled.

"I'm Jeri. Who might you be?"

"Ja-a-mie," he stuttered.

At that moment, my dog, Sandy, came into the room, and Jamie disappeared. It would be another several weeks or so before he reappeared, as he had a great fear of dogs.

When I next saw him, I was out riding my horse, Hook, in our arena. He was leaning on the arena fence, and I slowly rode over to him and dismounted. With a tentative hand, he reached out to pet Hook's silky white nose.

"Do you want to ride him?" I asked.

I wasn't sure how to help a spirit child onto a horse. What I experienced was me giving a leg up into the saddle to a child who wasn't physical, but sure felt that way. Reaching down, I cupped my hands together. I told Jamie to put his foot in my hands and then reach for the saddle horn. I then boosted him up into the saddle as he pulled himself up using the saddle horn for leverage.

Then around and around the arena we went, me walking alongside Hook and Jamie riding. A huge smile lit up his face. I tired out long before Hook and Jamie did. As I helped him down from the saddle, Jamie gave me a hug around my waist, which I felt just as if he were a flesh-and-blood child. Then he scampered off, gradually fading out of sight as he ran.

Even today, sixteen years later, I can't explain how exactly I was able to feel Jamie with my body when he didn't have one. I just know that I did feel him. Even today I can still feel, see, and interact with spirit children just as if they were still in their bodies. I no longer have a need to analyze how I'm able to.

Jamie's appearances were under his control, and he would just sort of pop into the physical dimension at odd times. He would appear while I was cooking or doing things around the house, for example. Mostly he was attracted to my horses and was always there in the arena when I was riding or working with them. I always found the time to give him a ride.

Kurt had left some model airplanes on his desk before he left for Iceland, and every so often, I would find Jamie playing with them as any physical twelve-year-old would, flying them around the room. Like all of the earthbound spirit children I've encountered, he could easily manipulate objects in the physical plane, even though he lacked a physical body. I saw both the actual model plane swooping through the room as Jamie held it in his hand, while his form passed through the furniture as if it weren't there. Jamie could spend hours on end focused on dogfights with invisible foes.

One day I decided to go down to the local hobby store and get an airplane-model kit for Jamie. If nothing else, I would put the plane together, and he would play with it. As I started down the first long aisle, I found myself thinking of Jamie and what model kit he might like. Within an instant, he was there beside me in the store aisle. Together we walked aisle after aisle, looking at different models and discussing the pros and cons of each. To an outsider, it must have appeared that I was a normal-looking person talking to myself! Two hours later, after finally deciding on the kit, glue, and paints, I walked out of the store alone. Jamie was on the porch when I got home, waiting anxiously for me.

Grabbing a stack of old newspapers, I spread them out, and Jamie and I began to put the model together. As the plane began to evolve, so did Jamie's story. He told me that his father had abused and eventually murdered him. Jamie did not know the dates he had lived and died, but from his description of the land and events happening around that time, I concluded his time period was around the 1930s. Jamie's father seemed to be a violent man when he drank "the whiskey," and he thought nothing of taking out his anger and violence on Jamie and his mother.

Jamie came and went several times during the next year. Then one day, he just disappeared. My hope is that he finally felt loved enough to cross over to the world of spirit and no longer be earthbound.

Mary, 1996

Mary was one of the most precocious of the spirit children I have had the opportunity to meet.

On our Idaho property, I kept a small hutch with two rabbits inside my goat pen. Every so often, I would come out and find the hutch door open and my rabbits loose. Luckily, they didn't run off. At first I just figured that I had forgotten to latch the door securely and reminded myself to pay closer attention when closing it.

Then one day I came out just as the door was opening and the first of the rabbits was jumping to the ground. The goats were lying down in the corner of their shed, just watching it happen. I mentally asked for whomever was there to come forth, and a young girl, maybe six or seven years old, appeared. There stood Mary, wearing the traditional yellow-gingham prairie dress with a white apron and a blue-gingham bonnet. She had long blonde hair and the most beautiful blue eyes I have ever seen.

Having encountered Jamie several times the year before, I started talking to the spirit girl as if she were a real child standing before me, for that is how she appeared. I asked her why she kept letting my rabbits out of their cage.

"I just wanted to hold one," she said.

Gathering up the first rabbit I could catch, while moving very slowly so as not to frighten her, I held out the rabbit to her to pet. I also showed Mary how she could open the cage and pet the rabbits while not allowing them to escape.

As the morning wore on, I asked Mary why she had remained earthbound for so long. With all the innocence of a child, she looked at me and said, "Because they haven't found me yet."

"Who hasn't found you?" I asked.

"Mommy and Daddy. They are still looking for me. I can't leave until they find me."

"Why are they still looking for you?" seemed an appropriate question. In response, I got the biggest roll of the eyes and look of exasperation, a facial expression I've seen numerous times from my own daughter.

"I'm lost, don't you know?" she said. "I ran away to chase the rabbits. There were so many of them, and we were playing hide and seek, and they would hop away when I would find them. But then they would stop and wait for me to catch up. I heard my mommy calling for me as it was time to leave, but I was having so much fun. Finally the rabbits all disappeared, and I didn't know how to get back to the wagon. I've been out here a long time, just wandering around. Then you came and brought these rabbits, and they were in the cage, so I let them loose so I could play with them again. I hoped they would show me the way home, but they never ran off like the others."

In Mary's mind, she wasn't dead; she was still alive and waiting for her parents to return and find her. I am not sure earthbound spirit children know they are stuck in this physical dimension. I believe linear time as we know it stops for them; they are just stuck or lost in one particular moment of time.

I spent a few more days talking with Mary, all the while researching how to offer spirits a way home to the world of spirit. Of the ways I found, the one I felt most comfortable with guiding them towards was "the Light from heaven," allowing them to cross over. Not having tried to use this technique before, I prayed hard that it would work and that Mary would be able to join her family in heaven.

A few weeks after I'd first met her, I went to Mary and explained, as best I knew, the truths and knowledge I had about crossing over into the world of spirit. I promised her it wouldn't hurt and that in a blink of an eye she would be home.

God is good and sends us angels and messengers when we need them most. As I spoke to Mary about crossing over, I wasn't alone. I saw the most beautiful angel come to carry her home. Mary wanted to take one of my rabbits with her. I didn't know how exactly Mary would cross over or what would happen if she were holding my rabbit, but I knew I had to trust that both of them would somehow be okay. So I placed the rabbit in Mary's arms. (Even though my rabbit was flesh and blood and Mary was not, I still saw this little girl holding the animal. Like Jamie, Mary was able to manipulate physical objects.) Then I said goodbye.

A huge stream of bright golden light opened up the sky and passed through the clouds. A rainbow appeared and surrounded all of us. There was such peace and love in that stream of colored light. Mary nodded to the angel, and in a flash, they were both gone. And there I sat, holding my rabbit. I knew I had been given a gift in seeing the rainbow bridge spoken of by so many others who communicate with the world of spirit.

I'll never forget that moment. Many years later, when I had my own near-death-experience, I felt that same golden light. Unfortunately or fortunately, depending on how you look at it, the rainbow bridge did not appear for me, and I didn't make the journey through a peaceful tunnel to the world of spirit. I was sent back to my body to complete what it is I came here to do in this lifetime.

Not long after Mary left, I came out to find the rabbit cage open and the rabbits hopping around on the ground. I smiled and heard the giggles I knew could only come from Mary, who was now safely home, in the world of spirit.

Children of the Sequoias: Ivan, Michael, Mary, and Homer

Our family's cabin in California's Sequoia National Forest sits on property that was once an active sawmill. It was built in 1937, and logging and milling got underway in this area in 1938. Tent and logging camps were set up, and the cabins currently used by various owners once housed mill workers and their families.

One evening, I could hear the pitter-patter of the rain on the cabin roof as my eyes swam in that time just before sleep—that time when I was there, but not there. Having just dozed off to sleep, I heard laughter and felt the mattress sink in places as four spirit children joined me on the bed.

"Who are you?" I asked as they gathered round.

"Ivan, my name is Ivan," said one, a dark-haired child.

"I'm Mary," smiled an elfin blond child, her eyes lighting up like shining stars.

"Homer," shouted a young man, who was taller and older than the rest.

"Michael," the fourth, a red-haired young man, said rather bashfully.

"We want you to write our story," said Homer, as he stood beside the bed. "We've come so you can write our story. You are a writer, aren't you?"

At that point in time, I was wishing perhaps I were not a writer. I was just a tired camper who desperately needed to go to sleep. But their young, eager faces, staring out from the depths of time, wouldn't let me give an answer that would disappoint them.

"Yes, I'm a writer," I replied. I assured them that I would write their stories in the morning, once I had gotten some sleep. Asking the angels to keep them safe for the night and offer them the Light for their journey homeward, if they chose to leave before I woke, I bid them all a goodnight.

A few hours later, as morning light broke over the surrounding mountains, I could still hear the rain continuing to fall. I awoke once again to see a sea of shining faces staring at me. Or perhaps they were just watching over me as I slept to ensure that when I woke, I would, in fact, write their stories. I was a captive audience, trapped on the bed and in the sleeping bag upon which all of them sat.

The rain finally let up, and the sun did its best to break through the morning fog coming off the mountain and into the quiet valley. The children and I gathered in the living room, so I could write by the light streaming in through the windows. True to my word, I took down their stories, and now I give them to you as they told them to me.

Ivan, 12 Years Old

I am earthbound. My dad and I went out hunting this morning, and somehow I got behind. And when I tried to catch up, I just couldn't find no trail or nothin' to follow. Finally I was thirsty, so I sat down by the creek out yonder to rest. Then I fell asleep when night came, and with it came the bear. I heard him, but I had no time to run, comin' out of a dead sleep like that. It was fast, death. After the first bite, I felt nothing, not even the shaking. I remember rising above my body and watching what was happening below.

Some dogs from the camp eventually found some of my bones and carried them back to camp. Pieces of my clothing were still attached—that's how they knew it was me. Everyone was upset and cried. Things got back to normal after they buried what was left of my bones. So why am I still here? Tell me, writer. Please tell me.

JC: Ivan, this is what I know about earthbound spirits: sometimes the death happens so quickly the spirit is just not ready to go and chooses to stay.

Well I'm ready to go; it's no fun here anymore. Too many people, all these cars—no one sees me. We knew you would see us, though. Jeremiah said you would. He's still down in the cabin below. He's havin' fun scarin' the people.

I have met with Jeremiah, the other spirit child Ivan refers to, on many occasions. Jeremiah is a tall, slender young man, approximately fifteen years old and wearing a set of dirty overalls. The cabin he prefers to "haunt" was once his home, and he is not ready to leave it. Each time I see Jeremiah, I offer him the Light and assistance if he wants to cross over, and each time he tells me, "Not yet, I'm having too much fun." And so he remains on earth by choice. He has assured me that he will contact me when he is ready to cross to the world of spirit, and I believe him.

Michael, 12 Years Old

River driving originated as a way for the lumberjacks to transport the logs from the woods to the sawmill. When the spring thaw came, the rivers ran high, and drivers, equipped with nothing but spiked boots and a piked pole, would roll the logs into the rivers and drive the mass downriver to the soaking/holding ponds, balancing themselves on top of the logs to keep them moving. River driving was the most dangerous work in the logging camp. Drivers could fall into the icy cold water and be crushed between the moving masses of logs, or they could get hypothermia from the icy cold water. Children of the logging camps were cautioned continuously not to play on the logs. Some listened, and some didn't. Michael was one of those who didn't listen.

I'm Michael. I passed from a log-rolling accident. You know how boys will be boys. We didn't listen to our pops, and anyway, Johnny dared us to log roll against him. I was winning, then Johnny slipped, and his log bounced into mine, and I went under. Those heavy logs kept right on movin' over me, and I couldn't push them apart enough to come up. It was dark down there, underneath all the logs. Guess we should have rolled them upstream more so they wouldn't have been packed so tightly in the soaking pond.

Mary, 13 Years Old

I'm thirteen. We [Mary, Ivan, Michael, and Homer] call ourselves the "merry band of four." There are more children here, but they don't play with us. They are much older. I passed with the fever. It was summer; you know how hot summers can be here. It came on suddenly, and the doc was down the mountain, tendin' to birthins. I was on the carousel when I passed, going round and round, up and down. Momma was by my bed, putting the wet cloth on my forehead. That is the only time the carousel would stop. Then I'd get hot, and it would start again. It got faster and faster, and I seemed to just lift off into space. Momma just kept puttin' the cool rags on my head even though I was gone. Poppa and the doctor finally got there the next morning, but it was too late. I miss them so.

Homer, 13 Years Old

I too passed of the fever, about the same time as Mary. It just seemed to sweep into camp and steal us away. Mary went first, and then others and I soon followed. It was fast and deadly. I didn't do a merry-go-round—that's a sissy girl thing. I climbed the mountain, higher and higher. I just kept going, so long as I could see the top; I just couldn't ever get there. I got tireder and tireder, and then I just fell all the way down. When I hit bottom, it was all over. It wasn't until later that they began putting those with the fever in the creek to keep their bodies cool. There wasn't a medicine to fix it, but the cool water seemed to give the body a chance to catch up.

It is possible that the fever that took Mary and Homer was scarlet fever, a streptococcal bacterium. A high fever around 101 degrees typically lasted three to five days. The younger the children, the more severe the fever. Antibiotics would not be used to treat scarlet fever until the early 1940s.

Later, I did as much research as possible to confirm Ivan, Michael, Mary, and Homer's stories, but came up empty handed. I believe, given the inconsistent recordkeeping and scant newspaper reporting of the time in which these children lived, their stories were not documented. I lived and communicated with the children's spirits, and I have no doubt that their stories are authentic. Ivan, Michael, Mary, and Homer could have been any of the many children that passed through the former sawmill town in the forest in the early 1900s.

The four children and I met again, and I helped them to cross over. The Light came down, and they all held hands and just disappeared into it. Jamie, who haunted the cabins, was there to watch them go.

3

Letters from Spirit Children Who Have Crossed Over

Each spirit child who came to me on the beach at Cape Cod in 2007 provided information they felt would draw their still-living loved ones to this book, where those loved ones could receive the message that the child was alive and well on the other side. All of the children chose to give only their first names.

While each child spoke, I asked him or her basic questions: (1) What is your name? (2) Do you know the date of your passing? (3) How did you pass? (4) What message do you bring? I left out those questions here, so as to not interrupt the flow of the children's messages, but I have included any clarifying questions I asked an individual child.

I allowed those children who wanted to sign their names to do so by physically using or manipulating my hand. Those signatures have been scanned into the end of the appropriate letter. Each is the child's signature, not mine.

What amazes me most about this sampling of letters is their recurrent themes. Each child speaks to the beauty of heaven, the desire to have their life and passing celebrated rather than mourned, and their ability to cross through time to reach out to their families and let them know they are still with them.

A Message from the Spirit Children

We, the children, have come together as one consciousness to bring forth our thoughts. The writer will hear our thoughts as a block of dialogue, comingled from us all, presented as one thought.

The presentation of our work, for we truly are the authors of our own stories and letters and messages, is in the format we have guided the writer to use. Our words, after all, are light and airy—on the wings of angels they arrive. There is nothing heavy about us, as we are vibration, energy, and spirit.

The writer has accurately represented us with her own words. Given the nature of how we come through, the writer is most accommodating. She allows us to be ourselves and bring forth our words without corrections for our mistakes in speaking.

In the spirit world, we are constantly speaking to you of the living world, hoping you will hear us and establish your own lines of communication. The writer shut us out during a period of her life while she searched to find balance in her world that was spinning out of control. The writer's cancer was the ultimate brake to stop the spinning, and we watched over her, biding our time until she was quiet enough to hear us. Once she remembered her "gift," we were able to speak with her again. There are so many children here waiting to send letters home, we are grateful that we are back and our words a part of her life, for we are the balance she so desperately sought that day on the beach counting waves.

We give you now, our writer and our letters, stories, and messages to share.

Aaron
June 20, 1983

My name is Aaron. I passed June 20, 1983. It wasn't by accident; it never is. Those who don't understand yet always think it is. They obsess over what they could have done, should have done, to prevent it. <u>There is no way to prevent it or change the outcome, for I chose this way myself.</u> We all do, consciously or unconsciously, knowing at the time.

I want my mom and my sister to know that I loved them more than life itself. There was nothing we would not have done for each other—nothing. Except my passing—only I could do that.

I am not "gone." I'm just not there in the physical body that you knew me in. I'm spirit now, and my body is healed and perfect. As spirit, I am able to be with you always, and I am. Susan, you have seen me many times, have you not? Mom, you have felt me ruffle your hair as I've done so many times before. I am watching over you and that mangy mutt of a dog, Poker Chip.

Heaven, the other side, is beautiful. There is much to do here. We continue to learn and improve by moving forward. And so must you, Mom; it is time to move forward, [to] get on with your life. Find forgiveness for those surrounding my death. They helped me to accomplish that which I set out to do in this lifetime. Forgive yourself for there was nothing, nothing you could have done to change the outcome. You were my strength and courage through it all. Do not hold onto resentment; release it, and let it fly free and away. Look for me next to you, for I am there. Celebrate my passing; do not mourn it, for I am truly one of the lucky ones.

There is so much sadness surrounding the passing of a loved one. There need not be. We are alive; it is our physical body that has died, not our soul and not our spirit. Celebrate us! Miss us, but know that we are but a thought away. Close your eyes and, in that silent space, see us and feel us. Reach out to touch us, and we will reach back.

Memorialize me if you must, but celebrate my life more. Reach out to other mothers and fathers who have lost their sons or daughters [and] help them to heal as I am helping you. Share with them what I have shared with you. Do an act of celebration of our lives. Release balloons, a million or just one filled with your love. We will be there to catch it as it floats into the air. Have a birthday cake with candles to celebrate my passing, for on that day I was reborn. Leave me love notes in that big bowl that takes up space. I will read them.

When you can find it in you to celebrate and move forward, then all will be well. All will be as it should be, and all will be right in this world.

We will meet again as we have done many lifetimes before. We are family from the beginning to the end of time.

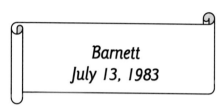

Barnett
July 13, 1983

My name is Barnett; I passed July 13, 1983. There is much to be said for passing over. It is truly beautiful here on the other side—"heaven" as you know it. Everyone I've known in my own life that has passed before me is here. I even recognized Aunt Molly, who I had only seen once but had heard so much about. It's like that here—you just know everyone; you feel it.

My passing was not in vain. I had done what I came to do, and it was time to move on. I will soon be back, different time, different place, and different face.

Do not remember my life in sadness; celebrate instead. We know we are the lucky ones because we have returned home. We do watch over you, and we are by your side always. We can hear you talk with us and tell us how sad you are that we are no longer there, but we are here. Close your eyes, expect to see us, and reach out. We are here.

I thank you for all you have taught me, the many life lessons, the hours of endless fishing when we caught nothing but the stories, the sharing of father and son. Move forward this day. Let the cloak of sadness fall from your shoulders. Lighten your load, always looking skyward. The angels surround you,

Mother; they are so beautiful. Father will be coming soon, but not yet. Let what time is left be spent in joy between you. It was not his fault. My passing was chosen, and [it] happened as it should. Remember your love in the early days. He [Father] was and still is your best friend. I love and miss you both. Thank you for being my parents and teachers.

Barnett

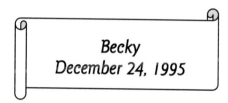

Becky
December 24, 1995

You guessed it: coming home from church on Christmas eve, a drunk driver—we were all gone in a second. There was an explosion and then angels everywhere. All of us taken together at once. We never even had a chance, the car was so mangled. Mom, Dad, me, and Johnny, just wiped off the face of this earth in a second.

I was supposed to have cleaned my room; I didn't. Who will take care of our house? Our pets? What will happen to all our stuff, my toys? I guess it doesn't matter anymore. We aren't there; we are here. Here is beautiful. There is love everywhere. We aren't still together as a family unit, though we do see each other often. We are working in different groups, preparing others for their own return to earth. I'm not ready to go back. It will be awhile.

Thank you for sharing, writer. Thank you for sharing. Oh, and merry Christmas. It is still Christmas, isn't it?

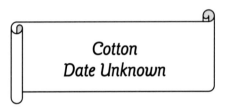

Cotton
Date Unknown

My name is Cotton. I don't know when I died; it was such a long time ago. My hair is blonde and short, like a bowl cut. That is how my mom always did my hair. I'm four feet, two inches tall. I'm that many years old. [He held up seven fingers.]

I didn't mean to disobey you, Mother. I just wanted to be up front where all the excitement was. There was so much going on, people everywhere. Suddenly I lost you and couldn't find you anywhere. I got scared and started looking everywhere for you. I never saw what hit me; I only felt it, but not for long. There was a beautiful angel with me. She reached out her hand, and I took hold. She told me not to look back, but I did. My body was there, still and silent. My angel carried me to heaven, Mother. When we got there, I looked back and saw that you had found me—my body, anyway. I'm so sorry, Mom. I promise to come back to you again, to be your little boy again. Watch for me, look in the baby's eyes, and you will see me, Cotton. You were right about the angels, Mom. They are everywhere. They are even with you now.

Heaven is beautiful, just like you described it. Kiss Amy for me and tell her I miss her. I do come and watch her sleep at night. That is what big brothers are supposed to do. That's what you taught me—to take care of those younger than I. I've lots of children to play with here on this side. Billy is even here. Remember Billy, Mom?

This time is short as I prepare to come again. Remember to look for me in the eyes. I love you, Mom. Look up—it's me, Cotton.

Cotton didn't sign his name because, he said, he had not learned how to "cipher." It is my impression that Cotton's passing occurred at a circus or carnival-type setting because of the background noise I heard as he was showing me what happened to him.

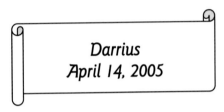

Darrius
April 14, 2005

My name is Darrius—D-A-R-R-I-U-S. Be sure to spell it right. My mom and dad won't know it's me, if you spell it wrong.

My passing was this date two years ago [April 14, 2005]. I knew it was coming, but they didn't; it was a surprise to them. I'd been sick for so long, I was tired. I just wanted to go home. I wanted to play and run free again. I had AIDS, and I was only seven. I was born with it, they say. My parents didn't come to see me much. There was so much that I couldn't do. Life wasn't fun. I spent most of my time in the hospital so they could care for me properly. The nurses and doctors became my family. Why did this happen to me?

The day I decided to go home, I had it all planned. I would slip away quietly in between bed checks. I wouldn't let on that I was leaving, but I would say goodbye to each of those who had cared for me as they came to check on me. I didn't get to play much with the other kids, but I would color a picture for them and for my mom and dad, just in case they came by.

The nurses always laughed with me when they came to change my bed. Or [they] would sit on my bed, and I would remind them to watch out for my angel. Her name was Glenda, and she was beautiful—just like the one in the story you used to read to me. [When Darrius says "you," I believe it is his mother he is speaking to.]

She was always with me. She said I was her special assignment. Glenda said she would be with me always, and we would cross the bridge together when I chose to go home. Glenda told me how beautiful it is there [on the other side of the bridge], how I will be free of pain and can run and play like a normal boy [there].

Mom and Dad, I kept waiting for you, but you didn't come today. You were going to; you told me you'd be here. I know you loved me the best you could. It isn't easy having a sick child that lives in a hospital. There are many of us here whose parents don't find the time for regular visits. I forgive you for missing this day.

It's time to go. I love you. I'm going home with my angel now. She says we will walk across the bridge together and I will be whole again, but mostly, I'll be home.

Evan
February 10, 1902

I'm Evan; I've been waiting a long time. I passed in February, 1902—the tenth. I know my parents aren't around any longer, at least not as I knew them. I was the first to pass, so maybe they had others [i.e., other children] after me. They were very young, my parents. Neither of them knew what to expect. I was born at home but caught the chill. I was so cold, and death was warm and welcoming. All I remember of my parents were their eyes. They were so deep and full of love for me. I didn't want to disappoint them. I thought I had a full life planned.

I just want to say that regardless of the circumstances, I loved my parents and wish I could have grown to know my brothers and sisters that came after me. We would have been the best family ever. There's no reason to mourn my passing, as it is beautiful on this side. I've lots of other children to play with. I'll be waiting for you, writer, when it is your time.

Mom and Dad are here now, as are Amy and Karen. Maybe we can play football when the boys get here. They'll be older, but not me; I'll always be a kid.

It's time to go now.

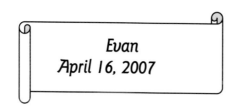

Evan
April 16, 2007

My name is Evan. [This is his nickname, not his given name; he said everyone calls him Evan.] *I missed out because I just got here two days ago. I was one of the students killed at Virginia Tech.* [On April 16, 2007, Seung-Hui Cho, a Virginia Tech student, went on a shooting spree at the university, killing twenty-seven fellow students and five teachers before killing himself.] *I just want everyone to know that there were many angels that brought us home. It all happened so quickly. There was no time to think about it. But Mom and Dad, my angels were with me, just like you promised. In the blink of an eye, we were here and gone. I'm sorry I didn't have time to call; I know how you like me to always call. I'm here with Grandpops; he met me when we crossed over. Oliver is here too!*

I know you will remember me, and I know you are very sad at this time. Please, Mom and Dad, celebrate my life, short as it was. Start a college fund for a less privileged boy to attend in my place. Let me be remembered that way. Remember, I told you I would go out in a blaze of glory, and I did. I know you believed me; you just didn't think it would be this soon. But I knew—deep down inside, I knew.

Share my things with this less advantaged kid: His name is Billy. You know where to find him. Mom and Dad, know that he isn't me. Don't make him feel like he has to fill my shoes. Allow him to be his own person. Just be there to help him along.

I've got to go now. This is all so new, and I had to jump in when I could to get this letter to you. I'll come in spirit and visit with you; just look for me and know that I'm there. Dad, play ball with Billy like you did with me; it will be good for both of you.

I love you both. Please, grow strong from this, not apart.

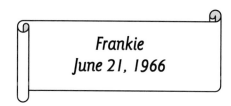

Frankie
June 21, 1966

Frankie, my name is Frankie. It's my turn. I passed on June 21, 1966. It was quick—very quick. One minute I was behind the wheel of my car, the next I wasn't. I don't believe the other driver ever saw me. I was sixteen when I passed. I left my mom and my dad and my sister and that funny dog, Buddy.

I am so excited to be able to give voice to my words once again. I just want everyone to know that I'm okay and I'm happy here. That seems to be what everyone wants to know— how we are and did we suffer. Heaven is beautiful, just as others who have passed described it. There was no suffering; my spirit was gone long before my body. I know my life was short and I didn't get everything finished, but I can come back again if I choose. I'd write about all that I've experienced since being here, but I want there to be an element of surprise left for when you come. We are busy for sure. Grandma is here and some man on Dad's side that I've never met—Cousin Ernie?

Mom and Dad, I know you are still sad, and I want to tell you to celebrate my life—don't mourn it. Julie has tried to tell you that I've come around, but you don't listen. Listen to her. I come for all the major holidays—Easter, Thanksgiving, Christmas. I even see you hang my Christmas sock and then take it back down, as you can't bear the pain or the memory. I am alive! We are just in another place, another dimension. There is nothing dead about us.

Dad, sorry I missed our annual fishing trip. I know it wasn't the same without me, but I'm glad you went. You needed to go to help you to feel closer to me. Just close your eyes and think of me, then see me. I'll be there. Julie can show you how.

Buddy passed over a short time ago (there is no "linear time" as we know it in heaven), and I was there to meet him at the bridge. I finally felt sorry for him; he was so old and fat. He's thin now and just like the puppy I knew him as.

I've got to go, there are so many others wanting to send letters home so their parents don't worry about them and feel so sad. When you meet other kid's parents who have passed, tell them please to celebrate the life of their child, no matter how short it was. We all wrote a plan before we came into this lifetime. We planned out what lessons I needed to learn on earth. Both you and Mom were there; did you forget, Dad? All is as it should be. I love you all; I've never stopped loving you.

Until tomorrow, my love always.

Frankie

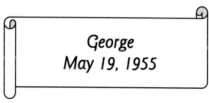

George
May 19, 1955

I wasn't going to come through; it has been such a long time since I passed. My father has joined me; my mom is hanging on, though she will be here soon. We will be a family again, as we were before. There is this grand vision that we all get together again up here and all is as it was on earth. That isn't totally so. We do know and recognize each other, but in a different view than physical. Soul level is how we know each other. Imagine a bunch of bubbles of light, for that is what we are—light energy.

I passed, as the train passed! I was pulled into the vacuum of the wheels as it went by. I was only five. Who would have thought I would be sucked in under the railroad cars as they whizzed by? That is why you are forever warned and cautioned to "stand back from the tracks." I am living proof that it happens.

Of course, everyone was horrified. We were all standing there, holding onto and waving our American flags. It was so fast! I was pulled into the angel's arms in an instant. My father and mother searched for my body, as it seems to just be carried *along with the train until they could get the train stopped. Such a happy occasion turned sad.*

I know it was hard for my parents to have anything to do with trains after I passed, given the circumstances. It wasn't the train's fault. Sometimes things like that just happen. I was only on loan for a short time to Mom and Dad. I just needed to know they were going to be okay again.

Take each day and be thankful for everything you have that day, for it can be gone just as quick.

Horace
June 25, 1961

"Horace here, move over," he says, pushing his way through the line of children. "Shot from behind by my older brother," he says, in answer to my question about how he passed.

They say BB guns are harmless, that they don't hurt anyone. That isn't true—I'm living (ha ha ha) proof that they can kill someone, as they did me.

We were out shooting at birds, my brother, Derek, and me. Derek was aiming at the nest in the tree I was pointing at when I felt a sting to the back of my head. At first it felt like I had been stung by a bee, and then I felt another sting. Turning around, I realized too late [that] it was Derek shooting me. It was the one that pierced my eye that took me down. I don't know what came over him, but Derek stood there laughing.

It wasn't until he saw the angel come that he got scared. I guess he thought I was just pretending. There was no pretending that day. It was too late. He was my brother, and I loved him; how could he do this to me? What had I ever done to him? They said it was an "accident." We all know it wasn't. Mom and Dad even suspected it wasn't an accident, but what could they do? Derek was their son also. In the end, they loved him the best they could; that is really all that anyone can do in the same situation. You do the best you can and pray for forgiveness.

Mom and Dad never had any more children. They were afraid to, in case something like this happened again. It is sad, because they were wonderful parents. The funny thing is, Derek went on to become a minister, a preacher. Sometimes good things come out of bad events. When it is Derek's time to come home, I will be there at the bridge waiting for him. After all, he is my brother, and I love him.

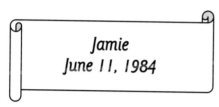

Jamie
June 11, 1984

Jamie, tell them Jamie is here.

No, I don't know when I passed. I was very young. Wait, Grandma is here. She says June 11, 1984. Grandma wants me to tell my mother that I love her and it wasn't her fault. Grandma says it wasn't my fault either. Child abuse is never pretty. Mom wouldn't have allowed it if she'd known it was happening. I tried to tell her; how could she not know? She saw the bruises; she just said I was clumsy. When her boyfriend would beat me, I'd just take my mind away. Sometimes I'd watch from above. I don't know how my little body would take it. His name was Jared, and he was a kind man when he wasn't beating me. What did I do to stir up his anger?

Then one day it was all over. He was so angry, and I was so small [that] not even my mom could stop him this time. The angels came and took me, and we walked across a beautiful bridge and into the light. Grandmother Ada was here to meet me. I never got to tell my mother goodbye and that I loved her. I'll come back again one day, when she has her life straightened out. I watch over her, though. There are many other children here just like me. We still don't understand how someone can be that mean so as to eventually kill us. Do you? Does anyone?

I asked Jamie if he would like to sign his name, and he responded: "No, thank you. I can't write yet. I was to start school in September. Mom had bought my school supplies. We hid them in a box under my bed. She still has them with my picture.

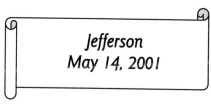

Jefferson
May 14, 2001

Thank you for allowing me to speak. Usually no one listens to me.

I am wise—wiser than most know. I too came to bring a message—a message about prejudice. I want to tell my brothers and sisters of all races, religions, and color [that] there is no inner difference between us. On the inside, we are all the same.

Look here, see these two eggs? One is brown on the outside and one is white. But when I crack each one of them open, what do you see? You see a yolk and slimy field of clear egg white. Same with a cow; [a] brown cow outside [is the] same as white cow or black cow inside. The only visual difference between us is our skin color. What is it that offends you about my color? I'm not different than you are; I was just born by a different-colored momma and daddy. That's all that is different. I work just as hard as you in school, if not harder, because the teacher thinks I'm "disadvantaged" because of my skin color.

I'm not disadvantaged; in fact, I'm even smarter than most of the kids here. I had to learn to read and write and do sums early on so I could set an example for the others—be a mentor of sorts. So why is it you felt the need to kill me? I was the same age as most of you. I did my best to be your friend, a friend to each of you. So why did you stone me? What did I do to you? Did my white color scare you?

Remember, the egg and remember the cow and the many other examples nature provides us with. We are all one. I forgive you all, for that is what my Jesus teaches: love one another as yourselves. I loved you. Why didn't you love yourself more?

JC: A very powerful message Jefferson, thank you for sharing. Were your parents missionaries?

Yes. Those we came to save eventually killed them. We are all together now. Color doesn't matter in heaven.

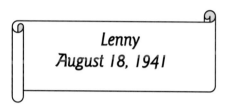

Lenny
August 18, 1941

I was shot, right at the end. I almost made it out alive. Almost wasn't good enough, was it?

I used to think I was never "good enough" until then. No matter what I touched, it all went wrong. I tried so hard to be good, to do what the others wanted of me, expected of me. It just never seemed to work out, though. I joined the army to prove them all wrong when they said I was a loser. I would have thought that still, until the day I got shot. I was lying there, bleeding, and I knew it was bad; I could hardly breathe, as if someone was sittin' on my chest. As I opened my eyes, I saw her—the angel. She was so white, and I was so bloody.

"No, don't touch me. I'll get blood all over you," I said, trying to make my hand shoo her away.

But my hand didn't move, nor did she. A radiant light shone all around her, and soon I felt it surround me. It was warm and peaceful. The sounds of battle disappeared into silence. She took my hand, and together we just left. I looked *back; my body was still there, [but] my eyes could no longer see.*

The journey home was quick, at least from my perspective. Blink, and you are there. I asked her why she came for me amidst all the blood and gore that litter the battlefield.

"You counted. You were 'good enough" was all she said.

I would learn later that everyone counts—everyone is good enough. We just aren't always taught that we all count in the eyes of God. We may do bad things, but in the end, we all count. That's the best message I can send back to earth: you all count.

It is my impression that Lenny was of German descent and was involved in the fighting between Germany and Russia.

Mark
Date Unknown

It's me—Mark. I don't know the exact date I passed. It was all a jumble, and everything happened so fast. It was a gunshot to the head. I was playing in my yard, and at first I just thought a bee had stung me. I'm afraid of bees. Bees make me sick, and I can't breathe. I tried to run to the house, [but] my legs didn't work, and I just tumbled into the grass. When Mom found me, it was too late. But this beautiful angel was there. She held my hand through it all. She held me in her arms and carried me into the sky. My legs didn't work. Up, up, up we went into the clouds. My mom, standing over my body, got smaller and smaller. When we finally stopped, we were in the most beautiful place. There were lots and lots of children there to greet us.

Johnny, my friend, is here. Mom, do you remember Johnny? Don't be sad, Mom. I miss you too. I'll be back to visit.

Johnny's going to show me how. I love you, Mom, and I know you love me.

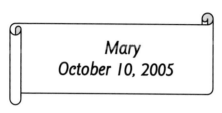

Mary
October 10, 2005

Mary—it is me, Mary. I'm finally here. Those boys kept pushing me out of line. Please tell Mommy and Daddy that I'm here. I'm okay, and it is so beautiful again. I hadn't been gone from home too long—just long enough to forget how beautiful it was.

Spike is here too. [She shows me her cat—a very big, fluffy, long-haired cat draped across her arms.] *We do lots of things together.*

I hope Mommy and Daddy will come visit me soon. I miss them both. They can leave Aaron at home, though. Sometimes he was so mean to me. He ran over Spike with his car, and then he ran over me. He was so angry that day. I tried to stop him from running over Spike; instead, he got us both.

Mommy and Daddy cried so hard. An angel came and took both of us here to heaven. [It was] so sad, what happened. Aaron is learning how not to be so angry anymore. I think he really did love me. I know I still love him, even though he was mean to me sometimes. There was an angel with Aaron too when he ran over us; he [the angel] was so sad, but he didn't bring Aaron with us.

I've got to go now. Just tell Mommy and Daddy how much I love and miss them.

Mary chose not to sign her name because she didn't want to put Spike down.

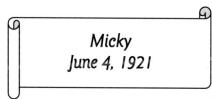

Micky
June 4, 1921

Do you not want my letter because it is so old? I know my parents are no longer there; in fact, they are here with me now. I just want others to know that once you arrive here, it is so much different than life on earth. No, we aren't floating around on clouds all day. It is hard to describe what we do other than to say, we just are here.

We spend time just "being" with God. It isn't boring or anything. I don't want to spoil the surprise for everyone, so I will just leave it to you to discover for yourself. I just want you to know, there is nothing to be afraid of here.

If you've been bad, or done bad things in your life, you can't imagine the forgiveness that exists in this place. You only feel guilty until you meet Him, and then He touches you, and it is all gone. How nice it would have been to feel that way on earth.

How did I pass? Gunshot to the back. Paralyzed me. I was just a vegetable. No good to anyone. Life didn't matter anymore. I just wasted away, on purpose. No one had time to take care of me, and I couldn't take care of myself. It was best this way. I just wasted away till I was nothing, literally. My heart just stopped beating.

An angel came for me; he was sad—I felt his sadness. There was little I could feel while alive, but I could feel his sadness. But when we arrived here, when the angel sat me down before Him, that sadness was all gone. He reached out and touched me, and I could walk again. I'm not paralyzed anymore. I have waited here for Mom and Dad to arrive so they could see me walk again. I can walk and run and take care of myself.

Micky, Micky—let's hear it now for Micky. Gotta run.

Nancy, 2003/ Sarah, October 10, 1909

Hi there. Jamie sent me over. I'm Nancy. I passed October 10, 1909, the first time. I was Sarah then. I was so cold and lost. The most handsome angel came to carry me home. He wrapped me in his wings, and I felt warm again. Then I was here. I chose to come back this time and came as Nancy.

I had wonderful parents. I was never cold again, like [I was] the first time. I felt such love from them, my new family. It was a car accident. Dad was driving, and the car came out of nowhere and just hit us. There was no way I could survive. I was so broken. Dad had a choice, and though our time together was brief, I told him that I would be okay. I'd been there before, but Mom and Danny needed him.

My angel came once again to carry me home. It's so beautiful here. Dad, don't be sad; it wasn't your fault. Learn to find forgiveness—that is all that matters. Not for me—for that man, for yourself. Only good can come from my passing. I love you all. I'm happy here.

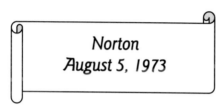

Norton
August 5, 1973

There wasn't much fanfare around my passing; I just did. I had been sick for a long time—pretty much from birth, though I had not been diagnosed during that first year. My parents thought something might be wrong, but small town, family doctor with basic learnin'. . . The headaches came daily, cutting into my brain. As a child, I didn't know what they were and just reacted to the terrible pain by screamin' and runnin', tryin' to escape them. I was labeled disruptive very quickly.

My parents were good folks. Mom and Dad both worked in the fields and did everything they could to make a proper livin' and provide for us. My older brothers oftentimes accompanied them to the fields while I stayed with Grandma Nell. When an episode would occur, Grandma Nell would hold me and rock me and sing me a song about Jesus, who loves all the little children. I wasn't thinkin' he even knew who I was then. Finally, the headaches got so bad the local doctor sent me to Iowa, to a doctor who specialized in children.

It was all a new experience for us. Mom and Dad came with me the first time. After they left me that day, I wouldn't see them again. It had been a long way, and we had to take several buses. It was a long walk from the bus station to the hospital, but we finally made it. No sooner had we arrived and sat down to cool off [than] an episode started. I was quickly rushed into the doctor's office and without Grandma Nell there to rock and sing to me, it hurt plenty bad this time. I tried to remember the words to the Jesus song, but the pain kept cuttin' into my rememberin'.

I was fed into a tunnel and told to lie still. How many of you know kids at the age of three who can lie still when their head is killin' them and they are in a huge machine that bangs and scares them? In the end, I imagined Grandma Nell holdin' me and rockin' me, and I was still as I could be. I guess it was enough. I didn't understand what the doctor was sayin', but it must have been bad, because Mom and Dad were both cryin'. I'd never seen them cry before. I didn't understand why. or what it was that was so bad. Somethin' that had to do with me, though.

I didn't go home that day; I never went home again except in my mind, when my head wasn't hurtin'. Mom and Dad never came back neither. It would be another few years before I would pass, but I didn't notice the time slippin' by. There were several kids whose parents didn't return. We just banded together and became a parent for each other. I kept askin' the nurses about my parents, but she just shook her head and said, "They couldn't get off work to come, but they love you." I guess I was costin' them a pretty penny.

Grandma Nell came twice. She would hold me and sing to me that song about Jesus. The kids that could would come sit on my bed when Grandma was there. She would tell us all stories and fill me in on what was happenin' at home. Things weren't goin' so well there; I guess it was better I was here. I sure missed everyone, though.

One night I heard the nurse whisperin' to herself, after she had changed my bag: "It's just a matter of time, such a shame." I guessed she was talkin' about me. I asked her the next morning if'n I was goin' to die soon.

"Yes," she said. "Yes, you are. But not today, not on my watch."

After that, I asked for her every day and didn't do well on the days she wasn't here. When you are waitin' to die, there isn't much excitement involved. I was afraid to close my eyes on those days, the days she wasn't here. Didn't know if I would wake up or not. No one taught me how to die, so I wasn't sure what I was supposed to do. Close my eyes and just go to sleep and never wake up? Or some clock goes off somewhere, and everyone shouts "time," and off I go? I didn't know how or when. I just knew it wouldn't be on Nurse Sally's day, because she had said so.

And it wasn't on Nurse Sally's day, in the end. In fact, after all the years of pain, my head just exploded in pain, and I was gone. That man Jesus that Grandma Nell always sang about, he came and took me. He was all white and shinin', and he reached out his hand. And when I took it, I was just gone from the bed. My body was still there, but I was gone, flyin' through space with Jesus. He does love all the little children. He came and got me himself. I was one of the little children Grandma Nell sang about. I was special.

Thank you, writer, for sharin' my story. I want Mom and Dad to know that I love them so. It's okay they couldn't come *see me. They did the best they could, and I know, I know, they loved me. It was better this way, they could remember me as the sweet boy I was—a bit disruptive at times, but still sweet the rest! They still come to the gravesite under the old elm tree—Mom especially. She talks to me a lot—tells me of all the hopes and dreams she had for me to be more than they were. She wanted the best for me. Maybe, in some strange way, that is what happened. Perhaps not the way she planned it, but perhaps the best adventure any boy could ever have, given the circumstances.*

I'm wiser now; I see things from a different perspective. It all works out in the end, doesn't it, writer?

JC: Yes, Norton, it does.

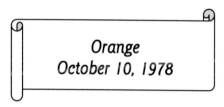

Orange
October 10, 1978

My mom called me Orange, said I was just round and orange when I was borned. I think my real name is Molly.

You are correct writer; I am from the hills—West Virginia, [the] Appalachians, "the Hollers." I am one of those Holler folk. Mom and Pop were very poor by most standards, but we got by. I don't think there could be more love in any family like there was in ours. Even though I was a surprise and another mouth to feed, I knew Mom and Pop loved me. On many a cold night, when the thin blanket barely kept off the chill, knowing I was loved got me though. See, this is what I know: without love you are truly poor. Love don't fill a stomach, but it warms the heart, and you can get through anything.

Huntin' accident took me this time. Me and Pops and Jed's boy had gone out huntin' early in the morning. Every morning there is a heavy fog that settles in the Hollers. A hunter uses it to their advantage to sneak up on the deer. We should have stayed together so we would know where each of us was. Instead, we fanned out. Pops went left, Jacob went right, and I stayed in the middle. There was a stream close by, and we knew this early in the morning the deer would be there. For me, I just liked to see how close I could get to them before they caught wind of me. I was almost to them when the blast rang out. I tried to run, just like them, but I was down and bleeding. The water was so cold. It was then I saw him, standing at the edge of the trees looking back at me. The biggest buck I had ever seen. His rack was magnificent, ten or twelve points at least. Perhaps he was the mysterious buck that others had talked of seeing. "Thank you" was all he said as he nodded his massive head in my direction. Then he turned and bounded off with the others.

By the time Pops found me, I knew it was too late.

"I saw him, Pops, I saw him, and his rack is as big as they say. He said thank you."

Pops just folded me in his arms. And then the angels came, and I just came out of Pops' arms and went with them, though my body stayed behind.

Mom and Pops, it is beautiful here. Aunty May is here. She met me at the bridge as we crossed over. There is so much love here, just like at home. I miss you, and I come often in your dreams. I feel you as you hold an orange close to your heart. Its okay, Mom, don't cry. Never let go of your love for me just because I'm not there to feel it. I do feel it—even way up here!

Orange said she didn't want to sign her name.

Paula
April 8, 2004

Give me a P!

  Give me an A!

  Give me a U!

  Give me an L!

  Give me an A!

  Who do you have? You have Paula!

  Of course, I know when I passed—April 8, 2004. Doing what I loved best—cheerleading. Home game, we were ahead. Danny had boosted me up on his shoulders. I'm not sure what happened next. I lay crumpled on the ground. It felt so cold. I couldn't move. Then I saw myself looking back at me. I was hovering above me, my body that is. There was no pain. There was a beautiful bright light that came down. We watched as everyone gathered round. I just lay there. "Mom, Dad, can you hear me?" I shouted, but my lips didn't move. I couldn't even feel their kisses or their tears. Poor Danny, he thinks it is his fault. I look right at him; can't he see me? "Danny, it's not your fault," I tell him, but I don't think he hears me.

So much activity on the field below. Even the game has stopped. Everyone is in a circle praying. It sounds so beautiful; all those prayers become music notes/chords sent skyward.

The medic is shaking his head now. I must be dead. But how can I be dead when I'm here watching?

"It's time to go," my angel said. As I took her hand, I saw a flash of brighter light, and we were gone.

Mom, Dad, all is well here. I watch you every day. Don't be sad, please. Help Danny to get through this time. He needs you. It wasn't his fault. How many times had we practiced and done that same move? It just happened, that all. Celebrate my life with a cheer as I have done here. I love you, and I'll be back again.

Give me a P-A-U-L-A

Peter
Date Unknown

To all the mothers and fathers who have lost children, I would like to come with a different story today. For those who want to believe communication is possible, but don't believe that they too can communicate.

Once upon a time . . . Isn't that how all your fairy tales begin? In a land far way . . .

How about instead: once upon a time, in a space close to your heart, a seed was planted—a small, nondescript-looking seed. I asked you to care for it by watering and speaking words of love to it each day. As the plant grew, buds appeared, and then one day, a beautiful blossom burst forth. You were so excited to see the blossom after your many months of care and communication. While you may have felt the communication was just one sided (you speaking to the plant), it really was much more.

The plant could feel the vibration of your voice, and it could feel the love with which you spoke to it each day. We are like that also. [Peter points to one of the kids in the circle.]

We can feel you, hear you, and see you. Each time you think of us, we are connected.

Why do you shake your head and go on? Why not just keep talking with us? We are that still, small voice you hear answering your questions. You may think it is just your imagination or your "self" that you hear, but really it is us, here in heaven, calling home without the use of a physical telephone, trying to connect with you.

While we are gone physically, we are here in spirit. We truly are one. Listen to your heart, not your head. Your head dwells in the land of fear; your heart in the land of love.

We are not "lost" or "gone" from you unless you shut us out and believe we no longer have access to one another. The point of my story is to tell you that we do have access, and it is through continued communication. You think of us, we respond, you hear/listen and respond back, and so it goes— dialogue with your son or daughter, mother or father, or beloved pet. I do not live in a land far away, for I am really here in your heart. Mom, Dad, are you listening? I love you.

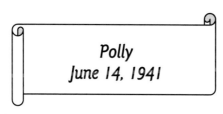

Polly
June 14, 1941

Why would anyone name their child Polly? Do you know how many times I heard "Polly want a cracker?" The boys especially thought it was funny.

War—I was killed during the bombing raids. The sirens went off, we ran to the shelter, but I stopped to grab my book. The next thing I saw was the angel and a bright flash of light. Then we were gone, just like that. Blink, and we were no longer there in the rubble and destruction of my home.

Mom and Dad didn't follow me, so I know they must be okay. I just want them to know I am okay and love them.

Writer, just tell them "auf Weidersehen"; they'll know it is from me. War makes orphans of us all, those alive and those that pass.

Polly also appeared to be of German descent. I believe both Lenny and Polly knew each other in their lifetime.

Priscilla
May 10, 2005

Before me stands a smaller version of Shirley Temple with curly blond hair, a red bow clip on the right-hand side of it. She has a flawless china-doll complexion. Priscilla is wearing a black and white checkered pinafore and shiny, black patent-leather shoes. The bodice of her dress is white, and she is wearing a gold, heart-shaped necklace and holding a floppy rag rabbit.

"Priscilla, would you like to say something?"

"Hi."

To say that Priscilla is bashful is an understatement.

"Do you know my mommy?"

"No, I don't know her, but I hope this book will find its way to her, so she will know that you are okay in heaven."

"Good. Mommy, I'm okay."

"Is that all you want to say?"

"Yes."

With that, Priscilla ran off to play with a group of children her age. I have no other details on Priscilla. If you are her mommy, just know that she is okay and with God.

Richard
September 15, 2006

I want to tell my story. I've been listening to everyone's stories. My, but aren't we a colorful bunch! We all have died and come to heaven. None of us have been perfect while in that last life, but we all made it here. It isn't so much about how good you are on earth as it is what is in your heart. Everyone has bad days; some are just worse than others.

I see our childhood as the testing years. We test everyone and everything. We are trying to figure out what this new world is all about. We are born into this lifetime incapable of anything but eating and pooping for the first few years. Then we get our wings—well, legs, actually, though it feels like wings because we become mobile and can move around.

Then we begin to learn all the dos and don'ts, of which there are plenty. From that day forward, it is nothing but learning where the boundaries are or even if there are any. If you grew up in a house where your parents set boundaries, then you learned a whole other set of lessons than those of us who grew up without boundaries, without lessons, without love and caring and support and encouragement. For many of us, *we were left to fend for ourselves, to find our own way from a very early age, in a very scary world.*

My parents were good people—at least they tried to be. Given all we went through, I think they did the best they could. They tried hard anyway. Let's just leave it there. I would have to say, looking around here and listening to the other stories, perhaps my parents were missing quite a few "social tools" and were doing their best to make do with what they had.

I was attacked and mauled by the family dogs. My parents lived in fear of losing what little we had, so they kept lots of big dogs. Red and black dogs, tall and lean and mean. The dogs always managed to be fed, [but] not always the kid. There were times I found myself stealing food from the dogs' bowl. Pretty sad isn't it?

I don't know how it happened. It was all so sudden, and Mom and Dad were there in the kitchen when it happened. I was just caught in the middle of it all. The dogs thought they had each other; really they both just had me.

Dad rushed me to the hospital, but it was too late. I had left my body, and the angel and I watched it all ride all the way to the hospital. There was so much blood, and Dad was so mad about it getting on the car seat. Seems like a small price to pay, for the loss of your son. The dogs are still at the old home place, but they are chained up now.

Earth is just an experience in learning lessons. You never get too old to learn new lessons. You spend your whole life learning the lessons. When do you get to live them? By the time you finally get them learned, it is time to die because you are so old and can't move around much.

Maybe we should be born knowing the lessons, then we [can] ease into them and start to live them our early adult years. That would give us plenty of time to experience all that goes with them.

Mom always taught me about consequences: do this, and that happens. For me, that was always bad. What if she had taught me just the opposite? Do this, and something good happens. What a different life I would have lived. What a different journey I might have had. Instead of teaching kids that bad things always happen, teach them that good things can also happen. Throw out all the don'ts and put in a lot of dos and see what a new life you might live. Oftentimes, we end up going down the wrong road because no one told us there was a right one instead.

For all the moms and dads out there reading this now, throw out your use of the word "don't" and introduce your children to that great word "do." Help them to dream dreams again and shoot for the stars. They can do it all if there is support and encouragement behind them. There is no reason for anyone to ever fail. They just have to choose the right road. The right road is the one where they get rewarded for being good and dreaming big. When the consequences of the don'ts come up, looming as big obstacles in their path, they know how to go around them and keep moving forward. They don't retreat; rather, they keep moving forward in confidence.

Life is good if you are taught to see it as good. Your living conditions can be horrible, but if you know there is another road out of there, it makes a huge difference.

Roy
November 11, 2002

I'm Roy. I deserved to die. I was so angry, and I took that anger out on everyone, especially my mom. She was doing the best she could to raise me after my dad left, but I cut her no slack. I wanted more. I said some mean and hurtful things to her. At night I'd hear her crying and praying to God for help. It just made me angrier, and I laughed at her. I'm not proud of it now.

A car hit me. I was yelling and screaming at her and ran right out of the house and into the street and blam! Splat! There I was, flyin' through the air. Mom saw it all. The last thing I heard was her scream.

Yes, there was an angel—a big black guy with wings! I was more afraid of him than I'd ever been of my mom. But he called me "Son" said it was time to go. He seemed to catch me midair, but my body fell to the ground. The driver got out to help my mom. Both were crying. At that moment, I felt all the anger dissolve away, then I felt numb. How could I have been so mean? My mom had only been good to me. She worked hard—two jobs just to make sure we had food to eat and clothes to wear. Why had I been so angry and mean?

The ambulance came, but it was too late, I was nothin' but a bag of bones. Somehow the guys were finally able to pry my body away from my mom. I had been so mean to her, and yet she still loved me and didn't want to let me go. Maybe her life will be better now.

I didn't understand then, Mom, but I do now. I just want you to know I'm not mean and angry anymore. Hard to be that way when there is only love surrounding you, like it is here. You tried to show me that; I didn't understand. I love you, Mom, and I want you to know how sorry I am for all the pain I caused you. I know you've forgiven me; now it's time to forgive yourself. I did this, not you.

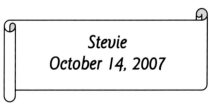

Stevie
October 14, 2007

Stevie was what I call a ragtag boy, with long black hair falling into his eyes, a runny nose, tattered jeans, and a ripped, light blue T-shirt. He was short for his age, which seemed to be about seven or eight years old. As he came pushing his way into the line of spirit children, I thought he seemed like the kind of kid everyone likes to bully.

"Just move," he said, pushing away Billy, another spirit child. "It's my turn."

With all the seriousness of an adult, Stevie sat down in front of me, staring deep into my own eyes.

Tell my mom I love her, I didn't want to leave her—I didn't. They made me do it—they made me jump. Those older boys were so mean, always pushing me to prove myself. I surprised them this time, though; I pulled Billy in with me. I hung onto his leg, and I wasn't letting go.

It was far down, and we fell fast. And it was just too deep. I tried to come up, but I just couldn't get there. I had no air left; I had to open my mouth. I don't remember much else. Somehow

I got here. Guess we died together, as there's Billy over there. Serves him right.

Are you going to see my mom? Tell her I miss her. I shouldn't have done it [jumped from the bridge]. I just wanted to get home, and they wouldn't let me pass. I'm just a kid; why do they pick on kids? Just tell Mom I love her, and I'll be back soon. I'm going to pick her again. Just tell her to watch for me; she'll know me—I'll have the same kind of heart. My heart was defective; that's why I didn't grow big and strong like the others.

I'm coming, Mom, I love you.

Stevie chose not to sign his name. As soon as he was done talking, he was up and gone after Billy again. Usually just the spirit children's voices come through, and I clairvoyantly perceive what they look like. This time, Stevie was right there, in my face, making sure I listened to him.

As for Billy, I could see him, but he didn't stop to give me a letter. He was just out to bully Stevie that day, just as he did when they were together in the physical.

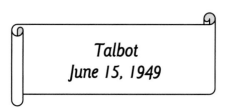

Talbot
June 15, 1949

My brother Jim is all that is left on earth. The rest of my family is here. Everyone wants to get his attention so he knows we are okay. He's not a believer. No one blames him for what he did. We just want him to know that. It is hard not to find forgiveness when you live in the land of forgiveness, as we do.

He shot me first, then Mom, then Dad. He even shot the dog. The dog never hurt him; why did he have to kill the dog? Why did he kill any of us? We tried to help him. Mom and Dad wanted to get him some help, but no one seemed to know how to help Jim. It was as if he was constantly fighting within himself.

I don't know if this letter will find its way into the prison system and reach my brother, but perhaps it will one day. Jim has to know that we all love him and have forgiven him.

Writer, do what you can, please, to find my brother and tell him I love him. He's my brother.

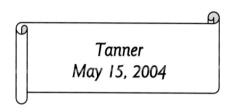

Tanner
May 15, 2004

Tanner here. I ain't gots no parents, least none I recognize. My grandma raised me till I run away. Couldn't take to no commandin'. Grew up just driftin' around this house, the next house, and so on. Never had no one home. Met some good peoples along the way. Guessin' that's why I'm here. I did something right at least once in my life.

I don't rightly know how I passed. Gang fight for sure, but it wasn't even my gang. Just everything went down all at once, and I was caught in the middle. Pretty quick for sure. Didn't have time to think about it. Everything just seemed to get out of hand and blow up out of nowhere.

I learned to survive by bein' involved in the gang. They taught me a way of life. Too bad I didn't have parents to teach me what I needed to learn. But it's cool. It's all cool. I'm not bitter. I gots a good home now, and everyone here is friendly. I'm not scared no more. I even have wings most days. Some days I lose them as I forget to be kind to another.

Mom and Dad would be proud of me if they could see me now. We're cool. When they get here, I'll see if they recognize me. Perhaps they will, perhaps they won't. I hope they look for me. What if they don't even look for me? They'll look for me. They are in heaven. Everyone looks for everyone they have lost. Hope they hurry, though. It's pretty quiet here, and I am ready for excitement. I spend a lot of time learnin'. That's okay too; good to know things—things that won't get me in trouble no mores.

Jams, just want you to know it is cool here, dude. Hang tough.

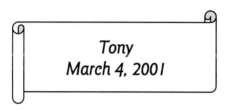

Tony
March 4, 2001

I was kidnapped. Horrible things were done to me, and then he killed me. He was a monster, sick and perverted. He enjoyed hurting me—he laughed each time I cried out. Death was welcomed, as it stopped the pain. The angel came and took me away. How could anyone be that hurtful to a kid? He killed the puppy too.

Mom told me never to talk to strangers. Most of the time I listened. I should have listened this time.

At first I was really angry. I fought the angel, as I didn't want to leave Mom all by herself. But I saw my body and the horrible things done to it, and I left. I think I cried all the way to heaven. I missed Mom so much. If only I could have said goodbye and let her know I was going to be okay.

Mothers, dads, brothers and sisters—don't talk to strangers! Mom was so right, and I'm so sorry I disobeyed her. Mom, I'm okay—really I am. I love you, and I watch over you, so be careful. Your time is coming soon enough; don't try to rush it. I'll be here waiting. I love you, Mom. Tell my story to anyone with kids; take it to the schools—everywhere there are kids. It happens. I'm living proof that you shouldn't talk to strangers, especially ones with puppies.

Walker (Johnny Walker)
February 2, 1959

Johnny Walker Red is what they called me. Can you guess why?

JC: You drank only Johnny Walker Red whiskey?

Correct. Lived, drank, and died from it. Before I died, it gave me life. Started early on. Watched my pop all the time I was growin' up. He always said, "It makes me a man, son'" So I followed in his footsteps, became a man early on. The Red gave me courage—courage to be stronger and more self-confident than I really was. Got me into bars and women long before my time. Made me popular with the girls, I was their fantasy bad boy, and they all wanted me. I used them, it's true. Then I met her, new girl in school.

She wanted nothing to do with ol' Johnny Walker Red. Tried to change for her. Tried to hide everything. Once Red gets ahold of you, he doesn't let go.

I got careless, crossed the line, all over in a matter of seconds. Me and the tree. I wish I could have been like that tree—strong, solid, and self-assured. It didn't even move when I hit it, but it sure mangled my truck. Looked like an accordion from above the scene. All that metal, the smell of gas—I scared myself right out of my body! There was someone with me. I couldn't see them; I could feel them, though. It was all so calm and peaceful. With all the destruction appearing below, I was actually at peace watching all of it.

There was the explosion as the gas tank exploded, and then I was here. They call it heaven. It's beautiful. Everything and everyone is at peace here. No one cares who I am; they just love me. Johnny Walker Red is gone; I'm just Johnny Walker now. Too bad I couldn't have been this way on earth, Missy was the sweetest thing. I know she was the one for me. Sometimes, it isn't good to follow in your pops' footsteps. I learned that lesson too late for this time around.

Mom is comin' soon; I've got to go meet her. We do that, you know?

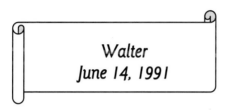

Walter
June 14, 1991

I want to tell my parents not to worry. I'm okay. I made it here safe and sound. And Julie—please tell Julie I'm sorry.

So many things happened so fast, it was all a blur. One minute I'm standing, and the next I'm not. The crowd just closed in on me. I don't think anyone saw me at first. My body was found much later. It was too late by then. I tried to hang on, but I just couldn't. It wasn't a bad experience, dying. At first I was afraid, but this warm light closed in around me and nothing mattered anymore.

I watched as I was carried away. People just kept stepping on my body. I could see it, but not feel their feet.

Mom, Dad, Julie, it is beautiful here, and I'll be waiting for you. Grandpa Jim is here; he's nicer to me now. I love you all.

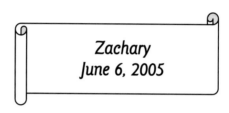

Zachary
June 6, 2005

Z-A-C-H-A-R-Y. Writer, why do you write the letters for us?

JC: Because you all have asked me to. I can hear you and share your messages and pray they reach your families.

Why should you care if our family knows?

JC: If I were a parent who had lost a child, I would want to know they were safe and with God in heaven. I can have faith and believe it all I want, but to have something tangible would be something to hold onto.

But you can see and hear us. You don't need anything to hold onto.

JC: That is true. I can see you, feel your presence, and hear your thoughts. But many others don't realize they can also see, feel, and hear you, so for them it is important to have something to touch.

Why is that, writer? Why don't they see, hear, and feel us? We are always trying to make contact to say we are safe and we miss them. If only they would just listen and trust their heart. We speak through our heart to their heart.

JC: I wish I knew the answer, Zachary. Our heart warms and loves us, and our mind protects us. Sometimes we just get it backwards. We forget what we knew as children. We lose our innocence as we grow up. We forget the days of magic, of knowing all that is truly possible between the world of spirit and the earth.

Well, writer, thank you for sharing our messages with others. Perhaps it will help them realize that we are only a thought away.

JC: Zachary, you are welcome. Ready to share your story?

Not much of a story exactly. I came, I stayed, and I went. No fanfare; no one missed my passing. I was just one of the lost boys, never knew a real home for long. One day I had a family; next week, I didn't. Saw inside of lots of houses, but never felt the warmth of a family to call my own. No one ever really cared about me or who I was, what dreams I had, who I wanted to be or to do when I grew up. My mom gave me away. How do you live knowing your own mother didn't want you?

JC: Perhaps she just couldn't take care of you and thought by giving you away, you would have a better chance at life. As a mother myself, I know it could not have been an easy decision. I want to believe she did it out of love for you, because it was the only way she could.

Look at me; does it look that way to you? I lived on the streets, ate from garbage cans, drank from the gutters or the fountain in the park. How could she not have offered me better? Anything would have been better than this.

JC: Zachary, did you pass on the streets?

Yes. Whoever said "There is honor among thieves" was wrong. I was killed for my blanket—a holey old blanket—by someone I thought was my friend. A blanket!

I'm safe now, and warm, and I have a family of sorts. Life is good, writer. Life is good.

4

Questions and Answers

The spirit children who wrote the messages in chapter 3 suggested this section. I put out a call to friends, asking for questions that the spirit children would answer. The questions to be answered were chosen by the children.

Do you miss your family?

Life on earth is very linear in that everyone does more "thinking" than "feeling." In heaven, we have evolved into a "knowing" attitude. We chose our family, our parents specifically, for we knew they would provide us with the environment in which to grow our soul. Having these specific parents and the family life, we knew, would provide us the opportunity to experience the lessons we needed to experience in order for us to grow and evolve.

We knew before coming to earth [into the physical world] all that would happen to us along the way. All those whom we have interacted with in the physical, we have interacted with since the beginning of time. This is our soul group, and we assist one another through many lifetimes, playing different roles along the way. Yet, as we aged, we grew further from the veil of knowing that separates heaven from earth, and we seemed to forget our plan. It was still written on our soul; we just consciously no longer remembered it. Thus, we struggled in the physical to remember the choices we needed to make along the way. Our soul remembered and guided us as best we allowed it to. Our exits (death, dying, and passing) were also up to us, and we were taken when it was time. We do not miss our family in the way that you still on earth would miss us. We have a love for the people that participated in this life lesson that surpasses that love that you experience in physical. But we are their best cheerleading section in heaven as we watch them complete their own soul growth. We do not miss them because we know we will be together again as they complete their own journeys [in the physical].

Do you feel sadness about your death? Do you have feelings about the sadness your death has caused your family?

How can one feel sad when to die is to live again in the midst of the Divine Spirit? While the physical act of dying may be fearful at the time, we are quickly reunited with the Creator of us all. There is no sadness but for the sadness we feel for leaving our friends and family who do not have the knowing that we are going to a much better place. Our physical death would be better off celebrated rather than mourned, for we are in heaven with the Divine Spirit. How could you wish for anything less?

Are you ok? Are you happy?

We are surrounded by divine love and knowing that truly does surpass all earthly understanding. We are better than okay and more than happy.

Did you arrive safely?

How could we not arrive safely when [we were] escorted across the rainbow bridge in the arms of angels?

What can you see around you? What can you see back in this physical world?

We can see everything around us and all that happens back in the physical world. There is beauty everywhere. We do not see ugliness or disabilities. We actually feel this great beauty and love because we are vibrating energy. There is no ugliness, only love.

From your vantage point now, what one or two things can we in the physical focus on to make ourselves better?

See the bigger picture. See your experience in physical as a way to overcome obstacles and obtain spiritual growth. Look for the divine love in everyone you meet. It is there, oftentimes buried deep and covered up by life experiences that have overtaken the soul of the person. But look deep within, with a knowing that if even a little speck of light could make its way into their darkness, it would be a beginning for them to find the love of the Father that the other person has forgotten.

Everyone you meet along your path is there because you have drawn them to you by thought, word, and action. Love is always your best choice in dealing with them. Show them love, no matter how hard it is. When your physical mind can't find it, let your heart and soul lead the way, for they have not forgotten the love of the Father.

The emotional wounds you suffered in this world—how do they feel now?

We do not remember the emotional wounds of your world, for we have risen above them. We called them forth as growth opportunities. Life and living are a two-way street, give and take. We suffered as much for you and your growth opportunities as we did for ours. Perhaps we came into your life so you could learn the lesson of forgiveness by way of wounds inflicted onto us. If you missed the opportunity to find forgiveness at that time, something or someone else will come again and offer you the opportunity, for that is how it works.

Where exactly is heaven or the world of spirit?

We see you struggle to search for a term that describes where we are at this moment. Your linear brain wants to name a place, a location where we exist. You see, we are spirit; we are vibrational energy—we are everywhere, in everything. We are. It truly is as simple as that—we are here, we are there, we are everywhere. There is no veil that separates us from your earth, for it is our earth also. Only you see us as needing to be separate, to be somewhere else.

Our writer sees through the veil; she perceives us as if we were in physical bodies, for it is easier for her that way. There is no actual separation; we are with you always, as you are with us. Your religious theology has made it necessary to have a heaven and a hell for its own purpose. Perhaps it would be easier for you to understand if we were to say that, upon the death of the physical body, the spirit, which is now vibrational energy and free of the physical body's heaviness, exists in a different state in the same atmosphere. Is that easier to understand?

In many ways, death of the physical body is much like crossing a rainbow bridge, for we experience a freedom that is truly free. We are excited to leave the physical body behind, and as we look upwards into the sun, we see the rainbow colors, prisms reflecting off the sun. For us, this is our bridge to home.

We hope this helps to clarify the confusion of where we exist. We are with you now, we can hear you now, we can see you now, can you see and hear and feel us?

How do you experience God or the Divine now that you are in heaven?

There is nothing so grand as the experience of God, the Divine Spirit, the Creator, the Father, on this side of the veil. We are truly one, at one, with the grandest architect of them all. We know only unconditional love here.

Does God intervene in our lives?

Not directly, no. He gave you the freedom to make choices and the knowing of what those choices might be to further your growth and bring you home to Him at your given time. He does send his angels to watch over you, for you are never alone. Even in your loneliest moments, He is there, as are His angels. He parted the Red Sea for Moses; do you not believe He would do the same for you? If you are drowning, He may send a log for you to grab onto. It is still your choice as to what you will do. Grab the log and ride it down the river, or drown because you didn't grab on.

Are our deaths—their time and their means—predetermined?

I believe we have five exit points along our life journey. We can choose to leave the earth plane in any of those <u>five exit points</u>. So while it may be the fourth exit point we had planned to leave on, if something happens along the way and we need/choose to leave earlier, we can take that opportunity in one of the first three exit points. Usually these exit points appear as an "accident" of sorts. We usually have a near-death experience at which time we meet God and He decides whether we stay or go. So there is a degree of choice to the matter as I see it. The example of the log and whether or not you chose to grab ahold or wait for a boat could be an exit point choice.

As the writer has said above, the life journey is for the growth of the soul, and lessons can be gained only by inhabiting a physical body for a time in the earth dimension. While one does plan his or her life journey from birth to death before coming into this lifetime, there are times when things happen that could potentially change the outcome of a predetermined destination.

To answer your question, no, there is no one sitting up here keeping track of when you have charted your death, and who in turn will send the bolt of lightning to strike you down if you don't leave at the appointed hour. If the soul determines it needs additional time to complete a lesson, it will go to Plan B or Plan C. The soul leaves the earth when it believes itself to have finished what it needs for its growth and not before. Sometimes lives are very short, but they are not without purpose.

Is there reincarnation?

"Reincarnation" is a word that your physical world has much trouble with. "Reincarnation" is a word that was used to describe a linear process that was not understood at the time. It was used by the early Protestant churches to control its masses

of people. If people believed they would come back into another lifetime, there would be no need to be good and follow church rule and doctrine in the first one. Therefore, it was spoken of in a negative connotation. Hindu and Buddists believe it to be when the soul or spirit comes back into a new life form— rebirth, oftentimes taking the form of an animal. Because [the Christian] religion does not allow for the return of a soul [to earth], except for Jesus' soul, there has been no word developed to accurately describe what transpires or the process. So let us not use the word "reincarnation"; rather, let us talk of soul advancement.

If you realize that physical lifetimes are your only opportunity to experience soul growth in the hands-on type of evolution, then the answer is yes, we return to physical. As spirit, which we are in heaven, we seek to learn the lessons of love and forgiveness that will advance our soul to its highest achievement: divine love. In the physical, one cannot conceive of just what divine love is, but we can learn the lessons necessary to evolve our souls to that attainment.

So yes, we come back many times, playing many different roles for the opportunity of others in our soul group so that we may all achieve the ultimate knowing of divine love.

Which, if any, of our human intuitions and hunches and subtle senses can we trust to be true?

Your heart, if it is not closed and hardened, can be your greatest barometer of where you are in your spiritual evolution. If it is closed, you need to open it up through forgiveness of those all around you, and then feel its love reach out to others every day. Through volunteer work that gives to another, your heart rejoices and sings. Love and forgiveness are the keys to unlock the mystery of knowing. Allow yourself to remember when you were spirit and to feel the love once again.

Will we be able to communicate with you?

Are we not communicating now? We just use the writer [to communicate] because she has remembered her gift and is willing to bring forth our words. You too can do the same. I am that still, small voice you hear inside your heart. Set the table, pour the tea, and know that I am there.

Will we see you again? Will you remember us when we come find you some day?

I will be here waiting when you are carried home by your angel. Your entire soul group gathers at the rainbow bridge to greet you and welcome you home when you cross.

You can see me now; you have just forgotten that you can.

How do you suggest we recover or practice our ability to see you?

You are taught that "seeing is believing." We say, "Believing is seeing." Until you believe you can see and hear us, you won't. It truly is that simple—believing is seeing. You want to make it so much harder on yourselves by believing you must be in a certain space at a certain time, doing certain movements or saying certain things, none of it is true. The simple truth is you already see and hear us; now believe that you do. Shall we talk now, you and us?

Do you know how much we, your loved ones still in the physical, love you?

Yes, we all know and feel how much you love us. There was never any question as to your love.

We understand that, as physical humans, you see life events differently. Physical life is our playground in which to evolve. Choices we make in spirit before coming into the physical are on purpose for both of us. If you are able to believe that everything that happens (good or bad, however you perceive the event) is on purpose for the souls involved, then our dying would be celebrated.

Sometimes our physical life is shortened for reasons beyond your conscious understanding. There is never to be any guilt attached to a passing. If you trust the Divine Spirit and know that all is as it was meant to be, then you can move forward. We ask forgiveness if this sounds harsh, but you served your purpose in giving us the time in physical that you did. Understand that our souls picked you to learn from in that brief passage. You gave us life in a different way. You are a blessing and will always be remembered for your strength and goodness.

Let us go, for we are where we need to be and have accomplished what we needed to accomplish. Do not mourn us—celebrate us! Feel privileged to have been a participant in the wonderful journey into physical that we experienced.

Some of you, including the one who asked this question, have allowed fear and grief to control your abilities to have other children come through them. That is not the way it was meant to be. There is nothing wrong with you; you have much to offer other children that may find their way to you. Let go of the belief that you are damaged and not worthy of bringing children into this world. Do not buy into the pronouncements of others that you can't get pregnant, etc. The only thing wrong is your thinking, your belief in a false statement given by another. Listen to your heart and cast out the fear. See your children as you would want them to be, and then create the energy between yourself and your partner that brings that child to you. If you continue to remember the fear, or guilt that you did something wrong, or the belief that it [the death of a child] will happen again, then it will be as it is now. See with new eyes,

new perceptions, and new beliefs, and allow heaven to work its
magic.

What signs do you look for to be able to communicate with earthbound receivers (such as this writer)?

*Openness—a willingness to put aside ego and judgment. One
who is able to put aside physical conditioning that says to not
believe in the possibility of hearing our voices. One willing to
hear us and record our words.*

Have you made contact with any other people in the physical?

*We have made contact with many others in the physical; most
just don't hear us. We are speaking all the time to those in our
soul group who are still in the physical. We constantly send
messages; sometimes they are heard, sometimes not. The soul
recognizes our voice, though, even if the physical body and
conscious mind are not listening.*

Have you communicated with other spirits there in heaven about this opportunity to send messages back to earth through those open to communicating with the world of spirit?

*It is widely known here of the capability to send messages back
to earth. Both we and you are all here together, just in different
dimensions of awareness. Spirit knows there are different
dimensions, and we see through the veil that seems to divide
them, while some humans can't get past their physical reality.
The veil is nothing other than a perceived physical separation.
Those who choose to communicate with you do so. There are
many advanced souls here communicating with others on the
earth plane who are open to spiritual communication.*

Is there an opportunity for you children or other spirits to communicate with earthbound spirits?

There is an opportunity if said earthbound spirit is willing. We are always encouraging the "lost ones" to reach out and take our hands and return home.

How do you locate other members of your soul family or physical family who have preceded you to heaven? How are you made aware of the location of spirits so you can find them? And have you found acquaintances or friends of the family there?

We exist now as vibrating energy—spirit. Our soul knows and recognizes other souls from many, many lifetimes together. There is no roll call of sorts that announces one of our friends or family getting ready to depart physical, so that we can rush down to the bridge and wait for them. [Smile.] "We know" is the only way we can express what happens here. We just know when their time is drawing near, and we wait. We have much to do once we return home, so it is not like we are involved with those on the other side all day long. But we know when you are coming, and we will be there to meet you.

Can you look down to earth and see what people are saying or doing about your memory?

It is not a matter of looking down at earth, for earth, the physical plane, exists in the same place as heaven. We just exist in a different dimension of that place. We do not see, as if with physical eyes, as you experience seeing; rather, we feel, we perceive the actions of others.

When some people go sit by gravestones or honor the remains of the earthly body, do spirits in heaven know? And, if so, are you able to communicate to those people?

We recognize that this ritual of visiting the gravesite in which our bodies have been interred is important to you in the physical. We do not understand why you go there to visit and mourn our passing when you could just as easily sit at home and celebrate a bouquet of flowers on the table in our memory. We are no longer in the ground. Our spirit is at home with God. We have risen above and beyond the grave. We will always speak with you on those visits; you will hear us if you are listening. Will you speak to us in return? If you celebrate us at your kitchen table or out in your garden, we will meet you there just as well.

In their messages, some of the spirit children mentioned that their pets are in heaven with them now. Have you met the spirits of other animals you knew in your lifetime on earth? (This might include pets you had, such as turtles, alligators, birds, cats, dogs, horses, or others.) And are they happy in their place in heaven?

We are all together here. We recognize each and every existence for which we have co-created together. While the physical appearance of our animal friends may have changed throughout our many lifetimes together, our souls will recognize one another on behalf of the last lifetime together.

What do spirits experience after arriving in heaven after an injury or malfunction of some part of the body on earth? For example, if a person was blind or deaf on earth, do they hear and see in heaven?

After arriving in heaven from our physical existence on earth, we are whole, we are complete, we are pain free. We are vibrating energy, we are spirit, and we are in the presence of God, the almighty. We are as pure as we can be. We take on, or assume, the characteristics you knew us to have in our physical life if you need that validation. But we are so much more. We are pure light and energy. We no longer need the heaviness of our physical bodies, for we assume the mantle of love and all its glory.

Once you, a spirit child, reach heaven, do you continue to age as you would on earth? Or do you remain with only the knowledge and years you had when you left earth?

Age and aging is a linear concept. Heaven is not linear. You will recognize us because we will look or seem to be as you knew us in our latest embodiment on earth. You will also know us as the different personalities we have shared with you in previous lifetimes. Our lessons on earth are woven into a much bigger picture of awareness and knowing.

Can you make contact with others there who might want their voices and stories heard?

Of course. Every soul, every spirit, is free to choose to communicate with others like the writer.

Do you have questions for someone on earth that you can convey to them through the writer?

Our questions would not be appropriate for the writer, only because we already know the answers. We came to earth having chosen a physical lifetime to learn and understand how and why there is such struggle on earth.

Instead of just trusting that there is a God who may go by many names, everyone has to find a way to make it a competition as to who is right or wrong. No one name is the only one. Everyone sees and experiences God in many different lights. What they choose to call their concept of God is pleasing to all. The writer grew up using the name "God." That changed as she grew spiritually, and she began using the names "All That Is," "Spirit," "Jesus," "the Father," and "Divine Spirit" to refer to the one she knows as God. Her road, her journey, has been different than another's journey, yet for her experience of God, the supreme being, the universe, the father and mother of us all, she has chosen the name that best represented her own knowing at that time in her journey.

You all seem stuck on there being only one name that is right! There are so many names that God is known as, all of them correct. For the Great Spirit knows our heart and recognizes His name when we call out to Him. It matters not what organized religion we are or by what name we refer to God. God truly is One to all and answers to every name by which His children call Him.

How much information do you want to share about your original locations on earth? That might help with getting your stories to the right people.

As explained by the writer, we have provided the information necessary to get our stories, letters, and messages to our families and to you, the readers, our friends. Spirit will lead them to find this book.

What happens to the spirits of babies who make it to heaven? What form do they assume? For example, if they were only eight months on earth when they passed, would their spirits be able to walk or talk?

As explained earlier, we return home as vibrating energy, as light, as spirit. We only assume our physical appearance for your benefit while you remain in physical. We are ageless and whole and complete upon our return home.

Can you talk more about the angels who come to earth to take spirits to heaven? How are they assigned *the task, and how do they know where to go?*

Well, you see, there is this big white board, and all your names are listed on it in colored markers. The angels line up and survey the requirements needed to bring you home, and then they pick and choose.

We are just playing with you! It is nothing like that. It is a privilege, an honor, to bring you home.

You actually have upwards of four angels by your side at all times, so someone always has an eye on you. The angels are advanced souls that no longer need to work out spiritual growth in the physical. They serve the glory of the Lord and are glad to do so. The angels are happiest when they see you progressing in a positive manner on earth and are just as eager to welcome you home.

Are angels former spirits who have a different job now that they are there in heaven? Were they previously beings on earth?

Angels are chosen by God to be entrusted with the gift of bringing you home. They are advanced souls, as explained in the previous answer. There are some guides (angels) who have come through physical lifetimes. In between physical lifetimes, spirits may choose to serve as angels and/or spirit guides helping those in the physical.

The writer is an example of someone who spent a lifetime prior to this one as a spirit guide. She was a guide for a woman who passed during the bombing of Hiroshima.

Do you mind answering these questions?

No, we do not mind answering these questions, for we see the thoughtfulness you have put into each one. We applaud your inquisitiveness and honor your search for higher answers. We are blessed to be given the opportunity to answer your inquiries.

In heaven, are there souls of people who have done wrong to you, or did they go to the other place? In other words, is everyone forgiven?

Everyone is forgiven. We each chose the roles we will play for the other's benefit and growth when participating in a physical lifetime. We understand on a deeper level what is required of us to bring about the lessons needed for soul growth.

It is not always easy to assume the role of a child abuser or a murder, for this is so against a soul's nature. We are all love from the core, and to override that love in order to be harmful to another is very hard. It is with love and understanding that we agree to take on a role like that for a physical lifetime. To go against the love, which we are, is so hard, but we do it for each other to learn the lessons of forgiveness and love.

There is no "other place"; there is only here. Your hell is what you live on earth. It is a linear fear concept used for control of those who don't conform to the teaching of one's society. God loves and welcomes us all home, because His message is for all—saints and sinners alike.

Why does growth have to be so painful?

Living in the physical is not designed to be painful at all. In fact, why would you come into physical just to be miserable? Rather, it is the choices you make along your journey that can create the painful vibrations. Your lessons are learned by the choices you make. No matter what choice you make, there are consequences attached to each. Those consequences can be painful or they can be joyful. Which do you prefer? Painful events can happen from your perspective, but in every event is an opportunity to see the event from a different angle. If you view your life from a "glass half-full (joy) or glass half-empty (painful) perspective, you will get just that. Always choose the choice that offers love as its answer. Life does not have to be painful unless you choose for it to be so. If you don't like how you are feeling, then make a different choice. It is as simple as that – make another choice.

If you have contact with another spirit who hurt you while you were both on earth, would that spirit apologize and ask for your forgiveness?

The hurt or harm is a physical action that takes place on earth. That is a lesson that is learned by both the spirit who inflicted the harm and the spirit that received it, and the lesson not always learned in one lifetime. Here in heaven, there is nothing but forgiveness.

Afterword
A Message of My Own

I awoke to the following words: "What you believe, it is your truth. There is nothing wrong with that truth. It belongs to you—it is your truth." These words ran through the ethers of my mind. Let me share with you now what I know.

I came into this lifetime to learn lessons for my soul's growth and evolution—lessons forgotten and, perhaps, lessons not learned before. Without lessons, our lives stagnate, and our souls do not grow. We do not evolve, and we go nowhere. Lessons can be painful, especially when they involve the passing of a loved one, be it a furry animal friend or a human being.

Thanks to the New Age movement, doors have opened for people such as me, who communicate with the world of spirit, to come out and be accepted in public. I was no longer shunned for what I did. At first, people searched me out to communicate with the spirits of their pets who had passed, yet many didn't believe I could talk with the spirit of their Aunt Suzy or Uncle Jim. Nor did they believe that they themselves could communicate with their loved ones.

Knowing I still have access to those who have passed from my life gives me hope that while physical death of the body is permanent, the soul and spirit live on, and the souls and spirits of our loved ones who have passed are only a thought away. I now celebrate a passing, rather than grieve. I am sad to see whomever it is go, but I know they live on in a much better place, and I will be reunited with them when my own time to pass comes.

Being a communicator has taken me on quite a journey. Speaking with the world of spirit is something I do for my own pleasure. Cancer helped me to see that being a communicator is who I am and what I do. It is my pleasure to bring forth these messages and letters because the children have asked me to share them with their loved ones.

Through my gift of communication, I have finally been able to put my own fear of passing to rest. There is no doubt in my mind that on the day I cross over, there will be a huge crowd gathered and waiting for me. I know there will be a room full of angels and spirits in various shapes, sizes, and forms to take me across the rainbow bridge.

I end this book knowing that I am a good person and that my gift of communication is just that—a gift. I am blessed to be able to speak to two worlds, the seen and unseen, and I am never alone. Nor are you, the reader.

Children clamber at the door of my mind so I can write their stories. I understand my life's purpose is to open that door and let them in. What you have just finished reading is God's seventh-wave answer to the question of my life's purpose. This is the first set of letters from the spirit children wishing to come through and speak. I am a communicator, and I am proud to be their writer.

I am gifted by God, and so are you. In your quiet space, just ask yourself, "What if this truly is possible?" Then count

until you reach the seventh wave, listening for God's answer.
May your own journey be as blessed as mine has been.

"Writer, are you there?"

About the Author

Jeri K. Tory Conklin is a native Californian, born and raised. She holds a master's degree in archaeology and anthropology, is a traditional Reiki master, and practices alternative healing techniques.

As a child, she began writing stories to entertain herself; now she writes for children, soldiers, and animals that contact her from the world of spirit. She is affectionately referred to as "writer" by those with whom she communicates.

Jeri lives with her husband and conglomeration of furry friends in Northern California. She can be reached at *seventhwavepublishing@yahoo.com*